Mansa Musa
Leader of Mali

Lisa Zamosky

Publishing Credits

Associate Editor
Christina Hill, M.A.

Assistant Editor
Torrey Maloof

Editorial Assistants
Deborah Buchanan
Kathryn R. Kiley
Judy Tan

Editorial Director
Emily R. Smith, M.A.Ed.

Editor-in-Chief
Sharon Coan, M.S.Ed.

Editorial Manager
Gisela Lee, M.A.

Creative Director
Lee Aucoin

Cover Designer
Lesley Palmer

Designers
Deb Brown
Zac Calbert
Amy Couch
Robin Erickson
Neri Garcia

Publisher
Rachelle Cracchiolo, M.S.Ed.

Teacher Created Materials
5301 Oceanus Drive
Huntington Beach, CA 92649-1030
http://www.tcmpub.com
ISBN 978-0-7439-0439-1
© 2007 Teacher Created Materials, Inc.
Reprinted 2013

Table of Contents

Mansa Musa

Mansa Musa (MAHN-suh MOO-suh) was an African king. The word *mansa* means "emperor." Mansa Musa ruled Mali (MAW-lee) from 1312 to 1337. During his years in power, Musa helped Mali to grow.

Mali is located in western Africa. It was one of the largest **empires** in the world at that time. Mali was at the peak of its power during these years.

In Musa's day, not many people traveled far from home. When they did, they brought back things from other lands. And, they told stories about the people they saw. Western Africa was one area that the rest of the world did not know much about. Musa would change that during his time in power.

◄ Musa was honored by his people.

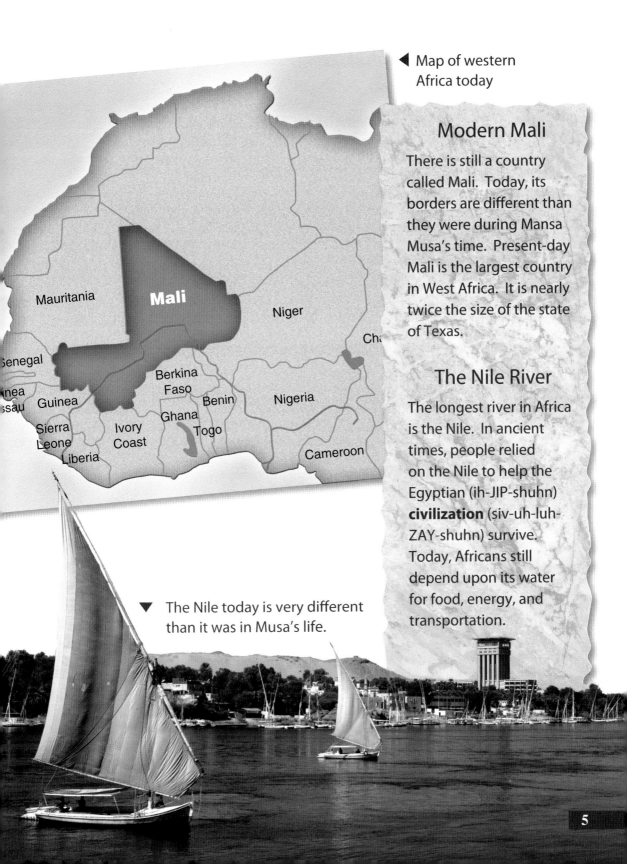

Mauritania

Mali

Niger

Ch[...]

Senegal

Berkina Faso

Guinea Bissau

Guinea

Benin

Nigeria

Sierra Leone

Ivory Coast

Ghana

Togo

Liberia

Cameroon

Modern Mali

There is still a country called Mali. Today, its borders are different than they were during Mansa Musa's time. Present-day Mali is the largest country in West Africa. It is nearly twice the size of the state of Texas.

The Nile River

The longest river in Africa is the Nile. In ancient times, people relied on the Nile to help the Egyptian (ih-JIP-shuhn) **civilization** (siv-uh-luh-ZAY-shuhn) survive. Today, Africans still depend upon its water for food, energy, and transportation.

▼ The Nile today is very different than it was in Musa's life.

Griots Keep History Alive

During Mansa Musa's time, people did not write about their lives very often. The events of a king's life were shared by **griots** (GREE-ohz). These people told stories about kings.

Africans shared stories orally for thousands of years. This was how most Africans learned about their history.

Arab **Muslim** (MUHZ-luhm) traders came to Mali. These men wrote the few stories that do exist about Musa. There are also some buildings, artwork, and statues left from his time in power. **Archaeologists** (awr-key-AWL-uh-jists) who visit Mali find these items.

▼ Ancient Africans wrote about their lives through pictures like these.

◀ This griot tells ancient stories today.

Modern-Day Griots

In Mansa Musa's time, each family had its own griot. Today, there are still griots in Africa. They play music or sing and dance as they tell their stories.

Just a Few Things

Only a few buildings, pieces of art, and writings from Mansa Musa's time are left today. **Historians** have found rock paintings in Mali that were done in ancient times. These pieces of art give clues about life in Mali during Musa's rule.

A Powerful Family

In Mansa Musa's time, there were **clans**. These were family groups who lived in western Africa. Clans lived together in small villages. Each clan had a special job. Some farmed, and others hunted.

Musa's family members were some of Mali's greatest leaders. He was born into a clan called Keita (KAY-ee-tah). This was a family of rulers. It was a very powerful family.

Sundiata (soon-JAH-tuh) was a very famous ruler of Mali. Historians believe that Sundiata was Musa's grandfather. Sundiata was very powerful. He helped Mali become a strong **kingdom**.

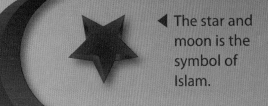

The star and moon is the symbol of Islam.

Musa was named Kankan Musa as a child. His name changed to Mansa Musa when he became ruler of the Mali people. Today, he's only referred to as Mansa Musa.

▼ Clans held meetings like this one to solve problems.

Grandfather Sundiata

Sundiata made an important decision for his empire. He chose to convert to **Islam** (is-LAWM). From then on, the Mali rulers were Muslims. Mansa Musa was the most famous Mali ruler.

Lion King

The lion was the symbol of the Keita clan. Sundiata was sick as a child. But he grew strong and became a powerful leader. He was known as the "Lion King." This name lives on as a symbol of his great leadership.

Growing Mali

Mali grew when Mansa Musa was king. He took charge of a large area of western Africa. Mali was close to the Niger (NI-juhr) River. This is part of the Sahel (SAH-hil) region of western Africa. This region is just south of the Sahara (suh-HAWR-uh) Desert. The Sahara is the largest desert in the world.

The Sahara is very hot and dry. So, it is difficult for farmers to grow crops there. But, it rains in the Sahel region. The Sahel region can get as much as 35 inches (88.9 cm) of rain in a year. Unlike the Sahara, food, fish, and animals grow in this region.

Niani (nih-AW-nih) was the capital of Mali. This city was near the Niger River. Timbuktu (tim-buk-TOO) was the center of Mali. Mansa Musa helped his empire grow in size and culture. He encouraged the arts, architecture, and literature.

Mauritani

Niger River

0 Kilometers 500

Miles 310

▼ The Sahara Desert

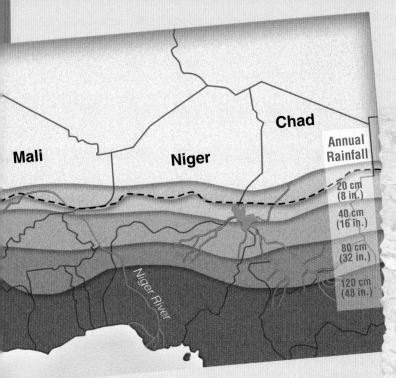

Mali

Niger

Chad

Annual Rainfall

- 20 cm (8 in.)
- 40 cm (16 in.)
- 80 cm (32 in.)
- 120 cm (48 in.)

Niger River

◄ This map shows how northern Africa changes from desert to farmland.

Musa's Empire

Mansa Musa's empire included present-day Mali. It also included parts of what is now Mauritania (mo-ree-TAY-nee), Guinea (GIH-nee), Senegal (seh-nih-GAWL), Burkina Faso (bur-KEY-nuh FAW-so), and other African countries.

Path to Travel

The Niger River is still important to Mali today. It is used for travel and trade.

▼ Life along the Niger River is busy, even today.

Trade in Mali

The great Sahara Desert separated Mali from the rest of world. Few people knew that Mali was on the other side of the desert. Arab (AIR-uhb) Muslims started traveling across the desert. They wanted to find places to trade.

Trade started to grow in the region. Soon, people learned that Mali had a lot of gold.

The people of Mali needed a way to **preserve** their food. It was very hot and dry in Africa. The food would spoil very quickly. Salt was one way of keeping food from spoiling. The people of Mali could not make salt for themselves.

Traders offered salt in **exchange** for gold. Mali was like other early civilizations in Africa. And, they were willing to trade the gold for salt. Soon, traders created trails across the Sahara. This made it easier for them to reach Mali.

▼ Long lines of camels carried salt along the desert trade routes in western Africa.

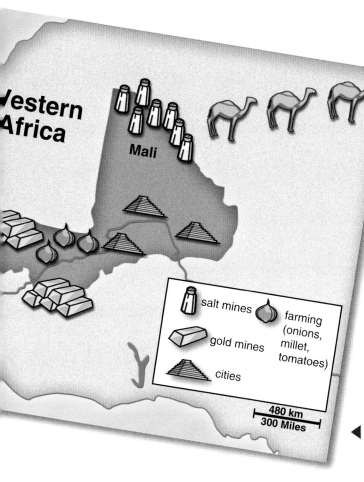

Western Africa

Mali

Map Key
- salt mines
- gold mines
- farming (onions, millet, tomatoes)
- cities

480 km
300 Miles

Still Trading

The trade that was strong between Africans and Arabs in Mali continues today. Salt is still a popular item.

Gold Mali

Today, Mali is still the third largest producer of gold in Africa.

◀ This map shows what items were traded in ancient Mali.

Ruling the Kingdom

Mansa Musa was in control of Mali from 1312 to 1337. There were millions of people under his rule. The empire was made up of many small **provinces** (PRAV-uhntz-es). Each had its own leader. These leaders answered directly to Musa.

The king had a special group of people to advise him. These men handled the important business of the kingdom. One **advisor** was in charge of money. Others were in charge of farming, fishing, and the forests.

▼ Farmers are very important to Mali today.

The most important advisor was Musa's griot. He kept track of events that happened in Mali. Musa did not speak directly to the people of Mali. He showed his power by speaking to them only through his griot.

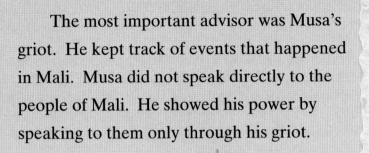

▼ This building has stood for hundreds of years.

Farming Today

Malians (MAW-lee-uhnz) still rely on farming for food and money. Eight out of ten people in Mali today are farmers.

Still Standing

Many of the buildings built during Mansa Musa's empire were made of mud. They were so well taken care of that some of them are still standing today.

Malian Religion

There were two religions in Mali. The Malian **traditional** religion was followed for a long time. It was very popular with people living in the countryside. The poor people in Mali also practiced this religion. Followers of the traditional religion believed that there was one God. And, God controlled everything. They also believed that there were spirits. Some were good and some were evil. People wore charms to protect themselves from the evil spirits.

◀ The Qur'an is the holy book of Islam.

Islam in Mali

Arab traders traveling from northern to western Africa introduced Islam to the area. Modern-day Mali is more than 90 percent Muslim.

Traditional Way of Life

There are still people in Mali today who practice the traditional ways of life. They do the same work their families have done since ancient times.

The second religion in Mali was Islam (is-LAWM). People who followed this religion were called **Muslims**. Muslims follow the teachings of the **prophet** Mohammed (mo-HAH-muhd). Muslims believe in one God. His name is Allah (AWL-luh). They study Mohammed's teachings in a holy book called the Qur'an (kuh-RAN).

These boys learn ▶ about Islam by reading the Qur'an.

◀ Traditional dancers

Keeping the Peace

Starting with Sundiata, most Mali rulers were Muslims. Mansa Musa was a Muslim. In fact, Islam was the main religion of the country.

Musa and other rulers in Africa knew that many people still followed the traditional religion. These people did not want to give up their old beliefs.

▲ Traditional Dogon (DOW-gawn)
dancers in Mali today

▲ Timbuktu

Great Thinkers

The University of Sankore (suhn-KORE) in Timbuktu was a center for Islamic study. It reached its height during Mansa Musa's rule. Muslims from all over the world came to the university to study. Today, the university has a collection of ancient papers. These papers show the actions and success of the people who have come to study and teach since ancient times.

Musa was a loyal Muslim. He was very religious. But, he needed to keep things peaceful within his kingdom. So, he also took part in activities of the traditional religion.

▼ Mosque at Sankore

Trip to Mecca

Many of the traders coming to Mali were Muslims. But, they were from the Arab world. They described the holy city of **Mecca** (MEH-kuh). Mansa Musa wanted to see the holy land. So, he decided to make a **pilgrimage** (PIL-gruhm-ij) to Mecca. The trip is also called a *hajj* (HAJ). Mecca is located in the country of Saudi Arabia. Musa decided to go to Mecca in 1324.

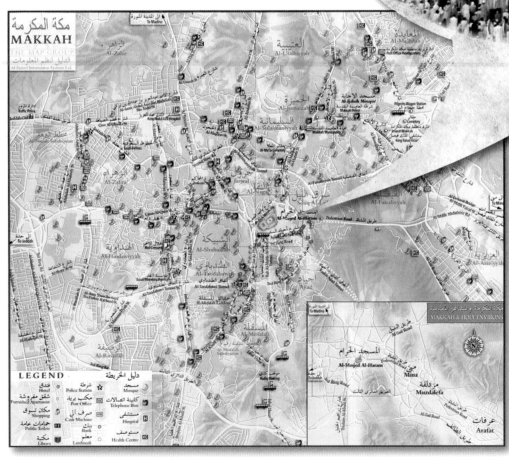

▲ The Great Mosque is at the center of Mecca.

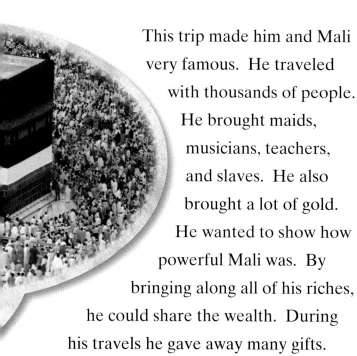

This trip made him and Mali very famous. He traveled with thousands of people. He brought maids, musicians, teachers, and slaves. He also brought a lot of gold. He wanted to show how powerful Mali was. By bringing along all of his riches, he could share the wealth. During his travels he gave away many gifts.

After one year of traveling, he arrived at the holy city. Musa's pilgrimage made him very famous. It also improved Mali's trade with the Arab world.

Reaching Mecca

There are no records of Mansa Musa's time in the holy city. He probably did the same thing that most Muslims do when they go to Mecca. Muslims visit the Great **Mosque** (MAWSK). They walk around part of it seven times. This tradition is the same today as it was long ago.

Camel Ride

Camels were used to travel during Mansa Musa's time. Camels do well in the desert. Dry heat does not bother them. Today, camels are still used to travel through the desert in parts of Africa.

Popular Mali

Mansa Musa's journey to Mecca was a success. On his trip, he made friends with rulers and traders. This opened new trade routes.

Musa hoped to increase trade by making Mali more of a Muslim nation. To do this, he invited important Muslims to Mali. A Muslim builder from Spain came to Mali. He improved the way buildings were made in Mali.

Musa also brought home four **sharifs** (shuh-REEFZ) from Mecca. Sharifs are very important in Muslim countries. They are relatives of the prophet Mohammed. Musa hoped that Muslim traders would come to Mali if sharifs lived in the area.

The trip to Mecca brought the king much power and wealth. People all around the world began to know who Musa was. This helped Musa increase the power of Mali.

Traditional mud ▶ mosque in Mali

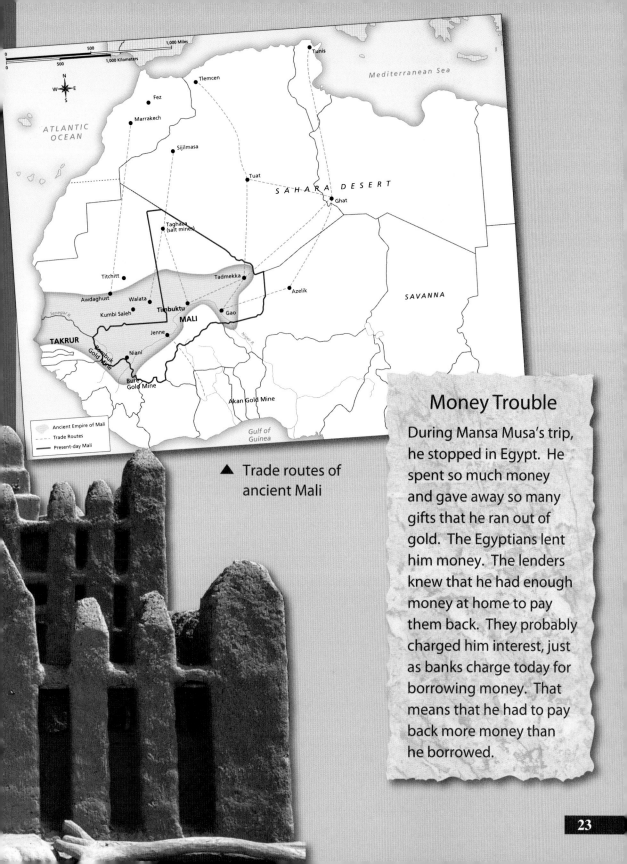

▲ Trade routes of ancient Mali

Map labels:
- 1,000 Miles / 500 / 0
- 1,000 Kilometers / 500 / 0
- N W E S
- ATLANTIC OCEAN
- Mediterranean Sea
- SAHARA DESERT
- SAVANNA
- Tunis
- Tlemcen
- Fez
- Marrakech
- Sijilmasa
- Tuat
- Ghat
- Taghaza (salt mines)
- Titchitt
- Tadmekka
- Awdaghust
- Walata
- Azelik
- Kumbi Saleh
- Timbuktu
- Gao
- MALI
- Jenne
- Senegal R.
- TAKRUR
- Bambuk Gold Mine
- Niani
- Bure Gold Mine
- Akan Gold Mine
- Niger R.
- Gulf of Guinea

Legend:
- Ancient Empire of Mali
- Trade Routes
- Present-day Mali

Money Trouble

During Mansa Musa's trip, he stopped in Egypt. He spent so much money and gave away so many gifts that he ran out of gold. The Egyptians lent him money. The lenders knew that he had enough money at home to pay them back. They probably charged him interest, just as banks charge today for borrowing money. That means that he had to pay back more money than he borrowed.

Building Mali Strong

Mansa Musa wanted to make Mali a better place. He felt that it was important to give people places to pray, study, and work. Musa is responsible for creating the first system of Islamic law. He built mosques, schools, and libraries. It was important for people to learn how to read and write. He wanted his people to be educated.

Art had a place in Mali's society, too. Performers could be seen dancing and singing in the streets of Mali. Weaving, pottery, and jewelry making were valued arts as well.

People from all over the world heard of Musa's trip to Mecca. They sent more traders across the Sahara. Mali's trade business grew under Musa's rule.

▼ Islamic mosques were built all over Mali.

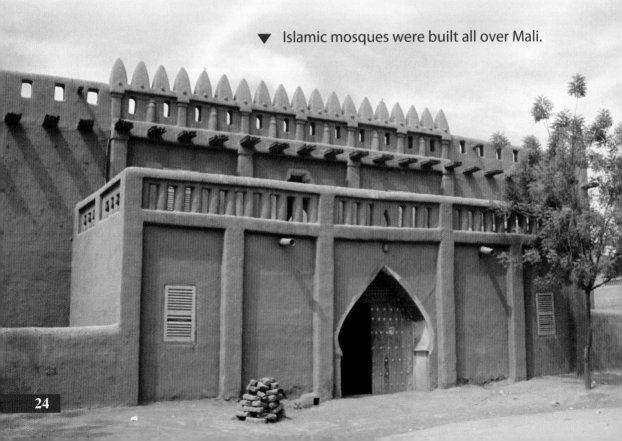

Muslims Pray

Muslims pray five times a day. If they can, they will go to a mosque at prayer time. Muslims always face toward Mecca when they pray.

▲ These Muslim children pray during school.

Education

Education was very important to Mansa Musa. He built schools during the time of his rule so that more people could learn. He is given credit for starting the tradition of education in this part of western Africa. Sadly, in Mali today, three out of every ten people cannot read.

▼ People in Mali take special classes to learn to read and write.

Death of Mansa Musa

When Mansa Musa died in 1337, Mali began to change. Musa had a son Maghan (MAY-guhn). Maghan took his father's place as ruler of Mali. But, he did not have his father's strength. Mali was attacked many times during his rule. Many of the schools and mosques built by Musa were burned.

Mali was growing weaker. At the same time, the Songhai (song-GAH-ee) kingdom was growing stronger. This empire was to the east of Mali. Over the next 150 years, Songhai became more powerful than Mali

▲ These are Songhai huts for storing grains.

▲ Grand Mosque

in western Africa. It remained powerful until about 1590. Sunni Ali Ber (SUN-nee aw-LEE BUHR) was a strong leader of the Songhai Empire. He expanded the kingdom to include Mali and other parts of western Africa.

Old Mosque

The Grand Mosque in Djenné (JUHN-nay) was built during Mansa Musa's time. It is still standing in Mali today.

Timbuktu

The city of Timbuktu was the center of trade during Mansa Musa's rule. Today, it is still used for trade by camel **caravans** (KER-uh-vanz) crossing the Sahara Desert.

A Great Leader

Mansa Musa was a great leader. He brought major changes to Mali and its people. He is responsible for expanding Islam in Mali. He built schools, libraries, and mosques for his people. He started a system of law that helped to govern Mali's society.

Through his travels, he made Mali a wealthy and powerful state. Musa brought attention to Mali. People from other parts of the world

▲ Mali today is a diverse, busy place.

knew of Mali because of Musa's actions. This increased the amount of trade Mali had with other countries. This is one of Musa's most important accomplishments.

Very little is left from Musa's time today. But, the things that are left remind people of what a great leader he was.

Instruments of Old

Some of the musical instruments used by musicians during Mansa Musa's time are still played in Mali today. The kora (KORE-uh) is like a lute. The *djembe* (JUHM-beh) is a kind of drum. These instruments have been in Mali since ancient times.

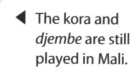

◀ The kora and *djembe* are still played in Mali.

Glossary

advisor—an expert who gives advice

archaeologists—people who study the past through artifacts

caravans—lines of people traveling together

civilization—culture created by a nation or a region

clans—large groups of relatives

empires—nations under the control of one ruler

exchange—giving one thing in return for another

griots—storytellers from Africa who share the traditions and history of a village or family

historians—experts who study history

Islam—religion started by the prophet Mohammed

kingdom—a region ruled by a king or ruling family

Mecca—the holy city in the Islamic world

mosque—a building where Muslims worship or pray

Muslim—a believer in the religion of Islam

pilgrimage—a journey to a holy place for religious reasons

preserve—to prevent from spoiling

prophet—a person who delivers a message from God or predicts the future

provinces—regions that are political units of a country or empire

sharifs—descendants of the prophet Mohammed

traditional—customary or usual way of thinking or doing things

Index

Image Credits